Psychology
Clinical

Adrian Collins

Adrian Collins

3

Copyright Page

First edition
All Rights Reserved
Author: © 2024, Adrian Collins

Index

Adrian Collins

Initial Clinical Evaluation

The initial clinical assessment is the crucial first step in the therapeutic process, as it allows the psychologist to thoroughly understand the problems faced by the patient and determine the best approach to their treatment. This process involves a series of steps and tools designed to obtain a clear picture of the patient's situation. It is not simply a casual interview; it is a structured procedure that includes key questions and the use of specific instruments that help to identify the origin and nature of the problems affecting the individual.

One of the most important components of the clinical assessment is the **initial interview**. This conversation between the therapist and the patient seeks to gather information about the patient's personal, family, social, and medical history. During this interview, the therapist not only pays attention to the answers the patient offers, but also to the way the patient communicates, body language, tone of voice, and the level of comfort or anxiety the patient displays. These elements are essential, as they can reveal information that the patient does not directly mention or is not even aware of that affects their well-being.

At this point, it is essential to establish a **trusting relationship**. A patient who feels comfortable with their therapist is more likely to openly discuss their emotions, thoughts, and behaviors, which will allow for a more accurate assessment. Therapists often use specific techniques, such as active listening and empathy, to make the patient feel heard and valued. This is vital, as patients who come to the consultation often feel vulnerable and need to know that they are in a safe, non-judgemental space.

The next important step in clinical assessment is the **administration of psychometric tests**. These tests are tools designed to measure various aspects of the patient's psychology, such as their level of anxiety, depression, cognitive functioning, and social skills. Depending on the nature of the patient's presenting problem, different types of tests may be used. For example, if a patient displays symptoms of depression, the therapist may administer a questionnaire that assesses the severity of their symptoms and how these affect their daily life. Psychometric tests provide objective data that complement the information obtained during the interview.

Another crucial element in this assessment phase is the **differential diagnosis**. Often times, the symptoms of one disorder can resemble those of other psychological problems. For example, a person with severe anxiety might have symptoms that are also seen in someone with PTSD or panic disorder. The therapist's job is to discern which disorder, or combination of them, is actually present. This is key, as an incorrect diagnosis can lead to ineffective or even harmful treatment.

A significant part of clinical assessment also involves the **exploration of contextual factors**. Psychological problems do not exist in a vacuum. The patient's life circumstances, family, work and social environment, play a crucial role in his or her mental health. For example, a person experiencing a recent loss or a situation of severe work stress may show symptoms that are directly influenced by these events. The therapist must consider these factors in order to have a complete and contextualized view of the patient's situation.

In many cases, the patient's **medical history** is also an aspect to take into account. Physical health issues, such as sleep disorders, chronic illnesses, or medication use, can directly affect the patient's psychological well-being. Often, the therapist may need to collaborate with other health professionals, such as physicians or psychiatrists, to get a clear picture of the patient's overall condition and how these factors may be contributing to their mental state.

The **treatment plan** begins to take shape from the initial clinical assessment. Once the therapist has gathered enough information, he or she can begin to outline a strategy for treatment. This might involve recommending a series of cognitive-behavioral therapy sessions, referring a psychiatrist for a pharmacological assessment, or even suggesting family therapy if the patient's environment is considered to be a major factor in their difficulties. The treatment plan is always personalized, as each patient is unique in their circumstances and needs.

Patient feedback is the final step of the initial assessment. Once the therapist has conducted a thorough analysis of the information gathered, it is important to communicate his or her findings to the patient in a clear and understandable manner. This may include an explanation of the diagnosis, possible causes of the symptoms, and a description of the suggested treatment plan. This discussion not only allows the patient to better understand his or her situation, but also gives him or her the opportunity to ask questions and express concerns. Collaboration between patient and therapist is critical to the success of treatment.

In summary, the initial clinical assessment is a complex process that encompasses much more than a simple interview. It requires a careful and meticulous approach to gain a clear understanding of the patient's problem and to design the most appropriate treatment. It is a balance between science and art: the science of psychometric testing and diagnostic techniques, and the art of creating a genuine and trusting connection with the patient so that they can open up and actively participate in their recovery process. This phase is essential to set the right course towards improving the patient's mental well-being, and lays the foundation for a strong and effective therapeutic relationship.

Anxiety Disorders and Their Treatment

Anxiety disorders are one of the most common conditions affecting people's mental health. They are characterized by constant worry, fear, or nervousness that is disproportionate to the situation that provokes them. Although we all experience anxiety at some point in our lives, especially in stressful situations such as before a job interview or an important exam, when this anxiety becomes chronic and interferes with daily life, that is when it becomes a disorder that requires treatment.

One of the most well-known types of anxiety disorder is generalized anxiety disorder, where a person feels excessive and persistent worry about a variety of things, from work to health to personal relationships, without a clear or specific cause. This anxiety does not go away easily and often causes physical symptoms, such as headaches, muscle tension, trouble sleeping, and difficulty concentrating. People with this disorder often describe it as a feeling of always being on alert or expecting something bad to happen.

Another type of anxiety disorder is panic disorder. This is characterized by sudden, recurring panic attacks, which are moments of extreme fear accompanied by physical symptoms such as palpitations, sweating, trembling, and in some cases, difficulty breathing. These attacks can be so intense that a person thinks he or she is having a heart attack or is going to die, which adds even more anxiety. Often, people with panic disorder develop an intense fear of having more attacks, which can cause them to avoid places or situations where they fear another episode might occur.

Obsessive-compulsive disorder is also a type of anxiety disorder. Although many people think of this disorder as a matter of "being very organized" or "having manias," it is actually much more serious. People with this disorder experience intrusive, repetitive thoughts, called obsessions, that cause them a lot of anxiety. To try to relieve that anxiety, they perform certain behaviors or rituals over and over again, known as compulsions. For example, someone may have an irrational fear that their hands are dirty all the time, and as a result, they wash their hands compulsively, even to the point of harming themselves. Even though the person realizes that their thoughts and behaviors are irrational, they cannot stop themselves from continuing to do them, which greatly interferes with their daily life.

Treatment for anxiety disorders, regardless of type, often combines psychotherapy and, in some cases, medication. The most commonly used and effective psychotherapy is cognitive behavioral therapy, or CBT, which focuses on changing negative thought patterns that fuel anxiety. In this therapy, a patient learns to identify his or her anxious thoughts and challenge the veracity of those thoughts. For example, if someone with panic disorder is afraid that a panic attack will kill him or her, therapy will help show him or her that although panic attacks are uncomfortable, they are not dangerous or deadly.

Another technique within CBT is exposure. This technique is especially useful for people who have phobias or avoid certain situations due to anxiety. It involves gradually exposing the patient to what they fear, in a controlled and safe way, until their anxiety subsides. For example, if someone has a phobia of flying, exposure treatment might start with talking about airplanes, then watching pictures of airplanes, eventually leading to being near an airport or even taking a short flight. The key is to do this gradually and with the support of the therapist, so that the person can face their fear without feeling overwhelmed.

In some cases, doctors or psychiatrists may prescribe medications to help manage anxiety symptoms. The most common medications are antidepressants, which are also effective in treating anxiety, and anti-anxiety medications, which are used to reduce symptoms in crisis situations. Although medications can be helpful, they are not considered a long-term solution on their own, as the most effective treatment is one that combines medication with psychotherapy. Medications can help a patient become calmer and more receptive during therapy, but the idea is that they can eventually learn to manage their anxiety without relying on them.

It's important to note that treating anxiety isn't a quick fix. It requires time, patience, and dedication from both the patient and the therapist. Often, people with anxiety disorders have lived with those symptoms for many years before seeking help, meaning their thinking and behavior patterns are deeply ingrained. Changing these patterns doesn't happen overnight, but with the right approach, most people can see significant improvement in their symptoms.

In addition to formal treatment, there are many strategies that people with anxiety can use to help manage their symptoms in their daily lives. These include relaxation techniques such as deep breathing, meditation, and yoga, which can reduce overall anxiety levels. Regular exercise has also been shown to be beneficial, as it releases endorphins, which are chemicals in the brain that help improve mood and reduce stress. Maintaining a structured daily routine and avoiding excess caffeine or alcohol can also be helpful, as these substances can exacerbate anxiety symptoms.

Finally, it is crucial for people with anxiety to know that they are not alone and that help is available. Anxiety disorders can make a person feel isolated or misunderstood, but they are very common and treatable problems. Seeking help is the first step toward a calmer, more manageable life, and with the right treatment, many people are able to regain control over their emotional well-being and quality of life.

Treatment of Depression

Depression treatment is a fundamental process to help people emerge from the deep sadness, hopelessness, and lack of motivation that characterizes this illness. Depression is not simply "feeling sad" or "having a bad day"; it is a serious disorder that affects the way a person thinks, feels, and handles daily activities, such as sleeping, eating, or working. Fortunately, there are several forms of treatment that have proven effective for most people who suffer from this condition. The appropriate approach will depend on the severity of the depression and the patient's individual circumstances.

One of the most commonly used methods for treating depression is cognitive behavioral therapy, or CBT. This type of therapy focuses on helping people identify and change the negative thoughts that fuel their depression. Often, people with depression tend to have very negative self-talk, where they criticize themselves, view the future pessimistically, and feel like they are a failure. In CBT, the therapist works with the patient to spot these automatic thoughts and challenge them. For example, if a person thinks, "I'm worthless, I'll never accomplish anything," the therapist can help them find evidence that contradicts that belief, such as past accomplishments or skills they possess but have overlooked because of their depressive state.

Therapy also focuses on changing behaviors that reinforce depression. Often, people who are depressed tend to avoid activities they once enjoyed or found fulfilling. This creates a cycle in which inactivity fuels further depression. In cognitive behavioral therapy, a common technique is behavioral activation, where the patient is encouraged to begin doing small activities, even if they don't feel like it. It can be something as simple as going for a walk, reading a book, or hanging out with a friend. The idea is that by engaging in enjoyable activities again, the cycle of inactivity and sadness will slowly break.

Another type of therapy that has been shown to be effective is interpersonal therapy, which focuses on relationships and a person's interactions with others.

Depression often affects how a person relates to others, either by becoming more withdrawn or, in some cases, more irritable and confrontational. Interpersonal therapy helps a person identify problems in their relationships and improve communication and conflict management. Sometimes depression can be linked to the loss of an important relationship, and this therapy can help a person process that grief in a healthier way.

For moderate to severe depression, antidepressant medications are often recommended. These medications act on neurotransmitters in the brain, such as serotonin, norepinephrine, and dopamine, which are out of balance in people with depression. Antidepressants can help reduce symptoms, such as persistent sadness, extreme fatigue, and lack of interest in daily life, but it's important to note that they are not a quick fix. It can often take several weeks before the full effects of the medications are felt, and in some cases, the dosage may need to be adjusted or a different medication may need to be tried before the right one is found.

It is important to note that antidepressants should not be seen as a "cure" for depression. Although they can alleviate symptoms, especially in more severe cases, they should ideally be combined with psychotherapy to address the underlying causes of the disorder. In addition, the medications should be prescribed and supervised by a doctor, who will assess potential side effects and ensure the patient is taking the correct dosage. Some side effects may include nausea, insomnia, or decreased sexual desire, but these are usually temporary and go away once the body adjusts to the medication.

Another approach that has become popular for treating depression is acceptance and commitment therapy, or ACT. Instead of focusing on changing negative thoughts, this therapy teaches people to accept their thoughts and emotions as they are, without trying to fight them. The idea is that the more we try to resist or suppress our emotions, the more power we give them. In ACT, the therapist helps the patient develop a healthier relationship with their emotions, allowing them to live a fuller, more meaningful life despite any negative feelings they may experience. Part of this process includes identifying the patient's personal values—that is, what is truly important to him or her—and then taking actions that are aligned with those values, rather than getting stuck in a cycle of emotional avoidance.

In addition to psychotherapy and medication, there are a number of lifestyle changes that can complement the treatment of depression. One of the most important is regular physical exercise. Exercise has been shown to release endorphins, which are chemicals in the brain that improve mood. Although it can be difficult to find the motivation to exercise when you are depressed, even a small amount of physical activity, such as a daily walk, can have a positive impact. Not only does exercise improve your mood, it also helps improve the quality of your sleep, which is often affected by depression.

Another key aspect is diet. Although there is no specific diet for depression, a balanced and nutritious diet can have a positive impact on mental health. Eating foods rich in omega-3s, such as fish, or antioxidants, such as fruits and vegetables, can help keep the brain healthy and improve mood. In addition, it is important to avoid excessive alcohol and caffeine consumption, as both can negatively affect mental health and sleep.

Social support is also crucial in treating depression. Often, people who are depressed tend to isolate themselves from others, which can make feelings of loneliness and hopelessness worse. Staying in touch with friends, family, or participating in group activities can be a big help. Even if you don't feel like socializing, the simple act of being around caring people can be comforting. For some people, joining support groups can also be helpful, as it allows them to connect with others who are going through similar experiences.

Finally, it's important to remember that recovery from depression is a process, and not something that is achieved overnight. There will be good days and bad days, but with the right treatment, most people can experience a significant improvement in their quality of life. The most important thing is to not lose hope and to remember that asking for help is not a sign of weakness, but a courageous step toward recovery. With the right support, depression can be treated, and people can feel connected to themselves and the world around them again.

Personality Disorders

Personality disorders are a group of psychological conditions that profoundly affect the way a person thinks, feels, and behaves. Unlike other mental disorders, which are usually temporary episodes or conditions, personality disorders are patterns of behavior and thinking that are inflexible and persistent over time. These patterns not only cause problems in a person's life, but also in their relationships with others, as the ways of perceiving the world and acting in it are often very different from what is considered normal.

There are several types of personality disorders, which are grouped into three major categories or "clusters" according to the main characteristics that define them. The first group, called cluster A, includes disorders that are characterized by strange or eccentric behavior. In this group, one of the best-known disorders is paranoid personality disorder. People with this disorder tend to be very distrustful, always thinking that others have bad intentions towards them, even without evidence to support it. This distrust can lead them to misinterpret neutral comments or situations, thinking that they are being attacked or criticized, which makes it very difficult to create healthy and stable relationships.

Another disorder in this group is schizoid personality disorder. People with this disorder tend to be very solitary and distant. They do not enjoy the company of others, nor do they seek to form close social bonds, either with friends or family. For them, social interactions are not important, and they often prefer to spend time alone. Unlike other people who may feel lonely or sad about not having friends, someone with schizoid disorder usually does not feel the need to connect emotionally with others, which can lead to a very isolated life.

The third disorder in this group is schizotypal personality disorder, which shares some features with schizophrenia. People with this disorder often have very unusual thoughts and beliefs, such as believing that they have special powers or that certain common events have deep meaning only to them. In addition, their way of speaking and behaving may seem strange or unconventional to others, making it difficult for them to fit into society or maintain close relationships.

The second group of personality disorders called Cluster B, is characterized by dramatic, emotional, or unpredictable behaviors. Within this group, one of the best-known disorders is borderline personality disorder, also known as BPD. People with BPD experience intense emotions that change rapidly. They can go from joy to anger or sadness in a matter of minutes, which often leads to very conflictual and turbulent relationships. In addition, they have a great fear of abandonment, so they can do everything they can to prevent others from leaving them, even if this means doing things they will later regret.

Another cluster B disorder is antisocial personality disorder. Often associated with criminal or morally wrong behavior, people with this disorder tend to feel no remorse for their actions, even if they have hurt others

They tend to be impulsive and have little regard for social norms or the rights of others, which can lead them to act in manipulative or aggressive ways. It's important not to confuse this disorder with someone who is simply antisocial or shy; people with antisocial personality disorder are often charismatic and able to manipulate others to get what they want.

In this same group we also find histrionic personality disorder, in which people constantly seek to be the center of attention. They often exaggerate their emotions or act very dramatically to get the attention of others. They love to be admired and often feel uncomfortable if they do not receive enough attention or are not the focus of the conversation. They can often be seen as superficial, as their relationships tend to be based on appearance and not on deep connections.

The final disorder in Cluster B is narcissistic personality disorder. People with this disorder have a constant need for admiration and an exaggerated sense of their own importance. They may believe that they are superior to others and deserve special treatment, which leads them to be very demanding and have little empathy for other people's feelings or needs. Although they may appear very confident, behind that facade they often have fragile self-esteem and are extremely sensitive to criticism.

Finally, in cluster C, personality disorders are characterized by anxious or fearful behaviors. One of the most common in this cluster is avoidant personality disorder. People with this disorder feel an overwhelming fear of rejection or criticism, which leads them to avoid any social situation in which they might be judged. They often feel inadequate or inferior to others, which prevents them from taking risks or participating in activities that could make them happy.

Dependent personality disorder also falls into this group. People with this disorder have an excessive need to be cared for by others and often rely on others to make important decisions in their lives. They are afraid of being abandoned or left alone, which leads them to be very submissive and go to great lengths to please others, even at the expense of their own desires or needs.

The final disorder in this cluster is obsessive-compulsive personality disorder, which should not be confused with obsessive-compulsive disorder (OCD), although they share some characteristics. People with this disorder tend to be extremely perfectionistic and controlling. They want everything done in a specific way and have difficulty delegating tasks or adapting to spontaneity. Often, their desire for order and perfection interferes with their ability to complete tasks or enjoy life, as they are always worried about everything being "just right."

Treating personality disorders can be challenging, as these behavioral patterns are deeply ingrained and have been present for much of a person's life. However, therapy, especially cognitive behavioral therapy and dialectical behavioral therapy, has been shown to be effective in helping people recognize and change dysfunctional behaviors. These therapeutic approaches focus on teaching skills to manage intense emotions, improve interpersonal relationships, and develop a more stable sense of self. In some cases, medications may also be helpful in managing associated symptoms, such as anxiety or depression.

It is important to remember that people with personality disorders do not choose to be this way, and often these patterns of behavior are the result of genetic and environmental factors. Empathy and understanding from friends, family, and therapists are critical in helping those with these disorders find healthier ways to live and relate to others. Although the road to improvement can be long, with the right treatment, many people manage to lead more balanced and fulfilling lives.

Bipolar Disorder

Bipolar disorder is a mood disorder that affects millions of people around the world. It is primarily characterized by extreme mood swings, ranging from episodes of mania or hypomania, where the person feels extremely happy, energetic, or even irritable, to episodes of depression, where the person feels very sad, hopeless, and lacking energy. These mood swings are not like the ups and downs that everyone experiences in everyday life, but are much more intense and can last for weeks or even months. For people with this disorder, life can feel like an emotional roller coaster, with very marked highs and lows.

There are different types of bipolar disorder, with the most common being bipolar disorder type I and bipolar disorder type II. In bipolar disorder type I, people experience full manic episodes, meaning the symptoms of mania are intense and can lead to very impulsive or risky behavior. During these episodes, a person may feel invincible, as if they can do anything. They may have a lot of energy, talk quickly, and make decisions without thinking about the consequences.

This can include spending large amounts of money, getting involved in dangerous relationships, or doing things they would normally avoid. Lack of need for sleep is also a common symptom, and sometimes people can go for days without sleeping but feeling completely energized.

However, this euphoria doesn't last forever. After a manic episode, people with bipolar I disorder may fall into a depressive phase. During this time, the feelings are completely opposite to those of mania. The person may feel extremely tired, unmotivated, and trapped in deep sadness. Things they once enjoyed no longer seem interesting, and they may have difficulty performing daily tasks. In more severe cases, these depressive phases can lead to suicidal thoughts, so it's critical to seek medical help if someone experiences these symptoms.

On the other hand, bipolar II disorder is a little different. In this case, instead of experiencing full-blown manic episodes, people have episodes of hypomania. Hypomania is like a milder version of mania, where the person feels euphoric or very energetic, but not to the point of losing control. However, these people also experience severe depressive episodes, which can be very debilitating. In fact, people with bipolar II disorder often spend more time in depressive phases than in hypomanic phases, which can lead to the diagnosis being mistaken for major depression rather than bipolar disorder.

One of the main difficulties for people with bipolar disorder is the unpredictability of mood swings. It is not always easy to know when an episode of mania or depression will begin, and sometimes these episodes can occur without a clear reason. This can make daily life very difficult, affecting the ability to work, study, or maintain stable relationships. Sometimes, people with bipolar disorder may begin projects with great enthusiasm during a phase of mania or hypomania, only to abandon them completely when they fall into a depressive phase.

Treatment for bipolar disorder often includes a combination of medications and psychotherapy. Mood stabilizers are one of the most common medications prescribed to people with bipolar disorder. These medications help prevent extreme mood swings and keep the person on a more balanced level. Examples of mood stabilizers include lithium, which has been used for decades to treat bipolar disorder, as well as other anti-seizure medications that can also have mood-stabilizing effects. In some cases, antipsychotics are also prescribed if the person is experiencing severe symptoms of mania.

It is important to mention that medication treatment should be supervised by a doctor, as adjusting dosages can be a delicate process. Some people may need to try different medications or combinations before finding what works best for them. Also, it is crucial for people with bipolar disorder to continue taking their medications even when they feel well. Sometimes, when a person starts to feel better, they may think they no longer need the medication, but this can lead to a relapse, as bipolar disorder is a chronic condition that requires ongoing treatment.

In addition to medications, psychotherapy is a vital part of treatment for bipolar disorder. Cognitive behavioral therapy, for example, helps people identify negative thought patterns and develop strategies to manage mood swings. It can also teach people to recognize early signs of a manic or depressive episode so they can take preventative steps before symptoms intensify. For example, if a person with bipolar disorder notices that they are starting to sleep less or feel unusually energetic, they can talk to their therapist or doctor about adjusting treatment and avoiding a full-blown episode.

Another important therapeutic approach is interpersonal and social rhythm therapy, which focuses on helping people with bipolar disorder maintain stable daily routines. One of the hallmarks of bipolar disorder is that changes in sleeping habits, eating habits, or daily activities can trigger episodes. This therapy teaches people to structure their daily lives in a way that minimizes these triggers. Maintaining a regular schedule for sleeping and eating, as well as avoiding excessive stress, can help stabilize mood and reduce the frequency of episodes.

Support from family and friends is also essential for people living with bipolar disorder. Often, loved ones may feel confused or frustrated by the person's behavioral changes, especially during episodes of mania or depression. That's why it's important for family and friends to educate themselves about the disorder so they can effectively provide support. Participating in family therapy can also be helpful in improving communication and understanding between the person with bipolar disorder and their loved ones.

Living with bipolar disorder can be challenging, but with the right treatment and support, many people manage to lead full and productive lives. It's critical for people with bipolar disorder to know that they are not alone and that there are resources available to help them manage their symptoms. The key is to recognize the early signs of episodes, follow the treatment recommended by health care professionals, and seek support when needed.

In summary, bipolar disorder is a complex condition that affects not only the person who has it, but also their loved ones. With advances in treatment and a greater understanding of the illness, more and more people can learn to live in a more balanced way, enjoying the good times and handling the difficult times with more control. As with many other mental disorders, the key to managing bipolar disorder is balance, both in treatment and in daily life, and knowing when to seek help before episodes get out of hand.

Post-traumatic stress disorder (PTSD)

Post-traumatic stress disorder, known as PTSD, is a psychological condition that can develop in people who have experienced or witnessed a traumatic event. These events can include things like serious accidents, natural disasters, physical or sexual assault, war, or even the sudden loss of a loved one. What defines PTSD is not just having gone through a difficult experience, but how that experience continues to affect a person's life long after the event is over.

When a person experiences something shocking or frightening, it's natural to feel scared, sad, or even have a hard time getting back to normal life for a while. With PTSD, however, these feelings don't go away over time. Instead, the symptoms of trauma can persist for months or even years, interfering with a person's ability to function in daily life. It's as if a person is trapped in the trauma, reliving it over and over again, even when the danger has passed.

PTSD manifests itself in a number of ways. One of the most common symptoms is intrusive memories or flashbacks, which are like reliving the traumatic event over and over again. These memories don't just come to mind in passing, but can be so vivid and realistic that a person feels like they're back in the middle of the trauma, as if it were happening right then. These flashbacks can be triggered by things that remind them of the event, such as sounds, smells, places, or even certain words. For example, someone who has been in a serious car accident may feel very anxious or panic when hearing the sound of brakes or driving near the location where the accident occurred.

Another common symptom is avoidance. People with PTSD often try to avoid anything that reminds them of the traumatic event. They may avoid places, people, or activities that in any way remind them of what happened. Sometimes, they also avoid talking about the event, as doing so can trigger intense emotions of fear or sadness. This avoidance may seem like a form of protection, but over time it can become very limiting to a person's life as they begin to withdraw and avoid situations they once enjoyed.

In addition, PTSD can cause changes in mood and the way a person views the world. Many people with the disorder experience feelings of guilt, shame, or hopelessness. They may begin to think that the world is a dangerous place or that they will never be truly safe. It is also common for them to feel emotionally numb, as if they can no longer experience joy or love as they once did. This emotional disconnection can affect relationships with friends, family, and partners, as the person feels distant and emotionally uninvolved.

Hyperalertness is another major symptom of PTSD. People with PTSD are often in a constant state of alert, as if they are always expecting something bad to happen. This can cause them to startle easily or feel nervous in everyday situations. For example, someone with PTSD may have a hard time relaxing in a crowded restaurant or may feel like they need to sit in a place where they can see the door and watch who comes and goes. This constant feeling of danger can be exhausting and seriously affect a person's quality of life.

Insomnia and sleep problems are also common in people with PTSD. Traumatic flashbacks, nightmares, or simply an inability to relax can make it very difficult to fall asleep or sleep soundly. This, in turn, can lead to other problems, such as chronic fatigue, difficulty concentrating, and problems at work or school.

One of the hardest things about PTSD is that it can feel very lonely. Often, people who suffer from this disorder don't want to talk about what happened to them, either out of fear of reliving the trauma or because they feel like no one else could possibly understand what they're going through. Also, people around them, such as friends or family, may not know how to help or may not realize the severity of the problem. This can cause the person to isolate themselves even more, which makes symptoms worse and makes it harder to seek help.

Fortunately, there are effective treatments for PTSD. One of the most common approaches is cognitive behavioral therapy, which helps people change the negative thought patterns that maintain the symptoms of trauma. In this therapy, the goal is for the person to learn to confront their traumatic memories in a safe environment, so that over time they are no longer as frightening or dominating. Relaxation and stress management techniques are also taught to help reduce symptoms of hyperarousal and anxiety.

Another therapeutic technique used to treat PTSD is exposure therapy, which involves gradually confronting the things the person has been avoiding. For example, if someone has been avoiding driving after an accident, the therapist might work with the person to gradually return to driving, in a controlled environment, until the anxiety subsides. By confronting the memories or situations that cause fear, people with PTSD can begin to regain control over their lives.

One form of therapy that has gained popularity in recent years is eye movement desensitization and reprocessing (EMDR). This technique involves recalling the traumatic event while performing specific eye movements guided by the therapist. Although the exact mechanisms of how this technique works are still being investigated, many studies have shown that it is effective in reducing PTSD symptoms.

In addition to therapy, medications can also be helpful in treating PTSD. Antidepressants, especially selective serotonin reuptake inhibitors (SSRIs), are often prescribed to help reduce the symptoms of anxiety and depression that accompany PTSD. These medications do not take away the trauma or cure the disorder, but they can make the symptoms more manageable, making it easier to participate in therapy.

It's important to remember that not everyone who experiences a traumatic event will develop PTSD. Some people can go through very difficult situations and recover without developing a psychological disorder.

However, for those who do develop PTSD, it's critical to understand that it's not a sign of weakness. Trauma affects people in different ways, and developing PTSD isn't something that can be easily controlled or avoided.

For those living with PTSD, the road to recovery can be long, but with the right treatment, most people can learn to manage their symptoms and return to living a full life. As with other mental health disorders, support from friends, family, and health professionals is key to recovery. Additionally, it's important for the person with PTSD to be patient with themselves and understand that recovery is a process, not something that will happen overnight.

In short, PTSD is a serious condition that can deeply affect a person's life, but it is not insurmountable. With the right support, people with PTSD can learn to confront their traumatic memories, reduce anxiety, and regain control over their lives. Although trauma can leave scars, it does not have to define the rest of a person's life. With time, healing is possible.

Eating Disorders

Eating disorders are serious psychological conditions that affect both the physical and mental health of those who suffer from them. These conditions are characterized by a dysfunctional relationship with food, weight and body image. People who suffer from eating disorders not only have unhealthy eating behaviors, but also experience very intense thoughts and emotions related to the body and food. These disorders can have serious consequences, both physically and emotionally, and require specialized treatment to be overcome.

There are several types of eating disorders, the most common being anorexia nervosa, bulimia nervosa and binge eating disorder. Each of these disorders has specific characteristics, although they are all related to an extreme concern with weight, appearance and food.

Anorexia nervosa is one of the most well-known eating disorders, and often one of the most dangerous. People with anorexia have an intense fear of gaining weight, which leads them to drastically restrict the amount of food they eat. They often view their bodies in a distorted way, believing they are overweight even when they are dangerously thin. This constant fear of weight gain can cause the person to go on extremely strict diets, skip meals, or engage in excessive exercise, all with the goal of losing more weight.

As the body is deprived of essential nutrients, the physical effects of anorexia become increasingly apparent. People with anorexia may lose so much weight that they develop serious health problems, including muscle weakness, loss of bone density, organ damage, and in extreme cases, death. Additionally, people with anorexia often isolate themselves from friends and family as their obsession with food and weight consumes much of their life.

On the other hand, bulimia nervosa is an eating disorder in which people experience recurrent episodes of binge eating, where they consume large amounts of food in a short period of time. After these binge eating episodes, the person feels extreme guilt and anxiety for having eaten so much, which leads them to engage in compensatory behaviors, such as inducing vomiting, using laxatives, or exercising in extreme amounts. This cycle of binge eating and purging can be very destructive to both the body and the mind.

Unlike anorexia, people with bulimia often maintain a normal weight or may even be overweight. This can make bulimia harder to detect, as it is not always apparent from the outside. However, the physical effects of bulimia can be devastating. Repeatedly induced vomiting can cause damage to the esophagus, serious dental problems due to stomach acids eroding teeth, and electrolyte imbalances that can affect heart function. In addition, people with bulimia often have a very complicated relationship with food, as they alternate between periods of restriction and binge eating, which reinforces their self-destructive cycle.

Binge eating disorder is another type of eating disorder in which people experience binge eating episodes similar to bulimia, but without the compensatory behaviors such as vomiting or laxative use. People with binge eating disorder often eat large amounts of food even when they are not hungry, and they feel out of control during these episodes. After a binge, they may feel extremely ashamed or guilty about overeating, which reinforces a sense of hopelessness and loss of control over eating.

Binge eating disorder can lead to the development of serious health problems, including obesity, type 2 diabetes, heart disease, and digestive problems. Additionally, people with this disorder often struggle with low self-esteem and depression, as they feel they cannot control their eating habits. As with other eating disorders, treatment is crucial to help the person break the binge eating cycle and regain a healthy relationship with food.

It is important to note that eating disorders are not just problems related to food or weight; they are complex disorders that involve psychological, emotional and often social factors. Many people who develop an eating disorder have an intense need for control, and food becomes a way of exerting that control over their lives. In other cases, the disorder may be a response to traumatic events or self-esteem issues. We live in a society that often values a thin body as synonymous with success or beauty, and this external pressure can play a role in the development of these disorders, especially in vulnerable people.

Treatment for eating disorders typically includes a combination of psychological therapy, medical treatment, and nutritional support. Cognitive behavioral therapy is one of the most effective forms of treatment for eating disorders, as it helps people identify and change the thought and behavior patterns that are contributing to their disorder. Through this therapy, the person can learn to develop a healthier relationship with food and their body, and to address the underlying emotions that are at the root of the disorder.

In some cases, a person may need to receive treatment in a hospital or at a specialist facility if their eating disorder has put their physical health at risk. These settings provide intensive medical care and monitoring to ensure that the person is receiving the nutrients they need while working on the psychological aspects of the disorder. In more severe cases, a multidisciplinary approach may be necessary, including doctors, nutritionists, psychiatrists and therapists.

It's important to remember that recovery from an eating disorder isn't something that happens overnight. It's a long, challenging process that requires time, patience, and support. People with eating disorders often face relapses in their recovery, but this doesn't mean they can't overcome the disorder. With the right treatment and support from loved ones, most people can learn to manage their symptoms and lead healthy, fulfilling lives.

The role of family and friends is crucial in the recovery of someone with an eating disorder. Often, people with these disorders feel misunderstood or alone in their struggle. Emotional support and understanding from loved ones can make a huge difference in the recovery process. It is important to avoid comments about weight or appearance, and instead focus on providing support and encouragement for the person to seek professional help.

In conclusion, eating disorders are serious mental health problems that can have devastating consequences if not treated in time. They are not simply a matter of vanity or wanting to lose weight, but complex disorders that require medical and psychological attention. With the right treatment and the necessary support, it is possible to recover and develop a healthier relationship with food and one's body. The key is to recognize the signs, seek help and not face the problem alone. With time and effort, recovery is possible and life can be much more than obsessing about food or physical appearance.

Autism Spectrum Disorder (ASD)

Autism spectrum disorder, also known as ASD, is a neurodevelopmental condition that affects how a person perceives the world and relates to others. The term "spectrum" is very important because autism can present itself in many different ways. Some people with ASD may need a lot of help in their daily lives, while others may be very independent. Every person with autism is unique, which means there is no one way to live with the disorder, and this is what makes ASD so diverse.

ASD primarily affects two areas: communication and social interaction, and patterns of behavior, interests, or activities. People with autism often have difficulty understanding social norms that come naturally to many. For example, they may not realize when it's appropriate to make eye contact, they may have difficulty understanding other people's body language or facial expressions, or they may not understand nuances of language, such as sarcasm or jokes. These communication difficulties don't always mean that the person with ASD doesn't want to socialize or interact, but they may find it difficult to understand how to do so in the expected way.

In addition, many people with autism may display repetitive behaviors or have very specific and intense interests. This may include making repetitive movements, such as swinging or clapping, or having a deep interest in a particular topic, such as trains, dinosaurs, or astronomy. These interests may seem very intense from the outside, but to the person with ASD they are a source of security and comfort, as they allow them to focus on something predictable and controllable.

Another common feature of autism is sensitivity to sensory input. Some people with ASD may be very sensitive to certain sounds, lights, textures, or even tastes. A loud noise that would be annoying but tolerable to most people may be unbearable to someone with ASD. Or, conversely, they may seek out certain stimuli, such as repeatedly touching soft surfaces or hearing specific sounds, to calm themselves down.

The sensory experience of a person with ASD may be very different from that of others, and this can lead to situations where they feel overwhelmed by their environment.

It's important to remember that autism is not a condition that can be "cured." It's a different way of being and experiencing the world. The goal of treatment and support for people with ASD is not to change who they are, but to help them develop the skills they need to live a full and satisfying life. Every person with autism has talents and abilities that can shine when given the right support. Some may be incredibly talented in areas such as math, music, technology, or art, while others may have an exceptional ability to notice details that others miss.

One of the biggest challenges for people with ASD, and for their families, is a lack of understanding from society. Because autism may not be visible to the naked eye, people often don't understand why someone with ASD may behave differently. For example, if a child with autism has a meltdown in a public place due to sensory overload, people around them may think they are simply throwing a tantrum or have no control over their behavior. But for that child, the experience can be overwhelming and out of their control.

Sensory meltdowns are common in autism when the person feels overwhelmed by their environment. These meltdowns are not an attempt to get attention or act out; they are a response to the extreme stress the person is experiencing. During a meltdown, the person may scream, cry, cover their ears, or even try to escape from the place where they feel overwhelmed. It is important for those close to someone with ASD to understand that these situations require calm, patience, and a safe environment for the person to recover.

ASD is usually diagnosed in childhood, although some people do not receive a diagnosis until their teen years or even adulthood. One of the early signs of autism is a delay in language development or social interaction. For example, a young child with ASD may not respond to his or her name, may avoid eye contact, or may show no interest in playing with other children. However, because ASD is a spectrum, some children with autism may develop language without problems, but may still have difficulty interacting socially.

Early diagnosis is key, as it allows the child and their family to receive the necessary support from an early age. Interventions such as occupational therapy, speech therapy and behavioural therapy can make a big difference in the development of social, communication and adaptive skills in daily life. The earlier a child's needs are identified, the better the long-term prognosis.

While ASD can present challenges, it is also an opportunity for individuals and families to learn to see the world in a different way. Diversity in the way people think, feel, and experience the world is a valuable thing, and people with autism remind us that there is no single "right" way to be human. Learning to appreciate and support the differences that autism brings is critical to building a more inclusive and understanding society.

Parents and caregivers of children with ASD also have a crucial role in their development. Raising a child with autism can be challenging, but it can also be deeply rewarding. As parents learn to better understand their child's needs and strengths, they can develop strategies to help them thrive in their daily lives. This can include creating predictable routines, offering sensory support, encouraging communication, and most importantly, showing patience and unconditional love.

There is now increasing awareness and understanding of autism, which is leading to greater acceptance and more resources for people with ASD and their families. Schools, workplaces, and communities are beginning to adapt to be more inclusive, recognizing that people with autism have a lot to offer when given the right support. Technology has also been a great ally, as many people with autism use technological tools to communicate and learn, allowing them to connect with the world in new and exciting ways.

Treatment for ASD is not one-size-fits-all; it must be tailored to each person's individual needs. Some people with autism may benefit from behavioural therapy, which helps them develop skills for daily living and social interactions. Others may need support in managing their sensory environment or handling complex social situations. Most importantly, treatment should focus on the person as a unique being, with their own strengths and challenges.

It is crucial that society as a whole understands that people with ASD do not need to "fit" into traditional expectations of social behavior. Instead of trying to make people with autism fit into a world that is often not designed for them, we should strive to make our world more inclusive and accessible. In doing so, we not only help people with ASD, but we also learn to value diversity in all its forms.

In short, autism spectrum disorder is a condition that affects how people interact with the world and with others. While it presents challenges, it also offers the opportunity to see life from a unique perspective. With understanding, support, and love, people with ASD can lead full and meaningful lives. Autism does not define a person, but it is an important part of what makes them unique, and that deserves to be celebrated.

Sleep Disorders and Their Intervention

Sleep disorders are problems that affect the quality, quantity, or timing of sleep, and can have a significant impact on a person's physical, emotional, and mental health. Getting a good night's sleep is critical to overall well-being, but when something interferes with the ability to get regular or adequate sleep, it can lead to a cycle of exhaustion, moodiness, poor concentration, and in severe cases, more serious health problems. Intervention or treatment for sleep disorders is essential, as improving sleep is one of the keys to maintaining good mental and physical health.

There are several types of sleep disorders, but the most common ones include insomnia, sleep apnea, restless legs syndrome, and circadian rhythm disorders. Each of these disorders has distinct characteristics, but they all have in common that they disrupt normal sleep and, as a result, can affect daily life.

Insomnia is probably the most well-known sleep disorder. It is characterized by difficulty falling asleep, staying asleep through the night, or waking up too early and not being able to get back to sleep. For some people, insomnia is an occasional problem, but for others it can be a chronic problem lasting for weeks, months, or even years. Insomnia is often related to stress, anxiety, or depression, although it can also be caused by other factors such as caffeine consumption, certain medications, or poor sleep habits such as spending too much time on electronic devices before bed.

Chronic insomnia can have devastating effects on a person's life. Not getting enough sleep affects memory, concentration, and mood, and can increase the risk of health problems such as heart disease, high blood pressure, and diabetes. People with insomnia often describe feeling trapped in a cycle where they try desperately to sleep, but the harder they try, the harder it becomes. The frustration they feel at not being able to sleep often makes the problem worse, as anxiety about not sleeping fuels the insomnia.

To treat insomnia, it's important to first identify the underlying cause. In many cases, making some changes to your sleep habits, known as "sleep hygiene," can make a big difference. This can include establishing a regular sleep routine, avoiding daytime naps, reducing caffeine or alcohol consumption before bed, and creating a relaxing environment in the bedroom. Additionally, relaxation techniques, such as meditation or deep breathing, can help reduce anxiety that contributes to insomnia.

In more severe cases of insomnia, cognitive behavioral therapy (CBT) for insomnia can be a very effective option. This form of therapy helps people change thoughts and behaviors that interfere with sleep. For example, someone who is worried about not being able to sleep can learn to challenge these negative thoughts and develop a more relaxed attitude toward sleep. Unlike sleep medications, which often only offer a temporary solution, CBT provides long-term tools to improve sleep quality.

Another common sleep disorder is sleep apnea. This disorder occurs when a person's breathing is repeatedly interrupted during sleep. People with sleep apnea often don't realize that they stop breathing during the night, but their bed partners often notice that they snore loudly or have pauses in breathing. Sleep apnea can be very dangerous, as it deprives the body of oxygen, which can lead to heart problems, high blood pressure, and other health issues.

The most common treatment for sleep apnea is the use of a device called CPAP (continuous positive airway pressure). This device keeps the airway open while a person sleeps, which helps prevent interruptions in breathing. Although it may take some time to get used to using CPAP, many people with sleep apnea find that it greatly improves the quality of their sleep and their overall health. In addition to CPAP, some lifestyle changes, such as losing weight or avoiding alcohol, may also be helpful in reducing sleep apnea symptoms.

Restless legs syndrome is another sleep disorder that can severely impact the quality of rest. People with this syndrome feel an uncontrollable urge to move their legs while they are resting, especially at night. This sensation can be uncomfortable or even painful, interfering with the ability to fall asleep. The causes of restless legs syndrome are not fully understood, but it is thought to be related to an imbalance in the levels of dopamine in the brain, which is a chemical that regulates movement.

Treatment for restless legs syndrome may include medications that increase dopamine levels, as well as lifestyle changes. Avoiding caffeine and alcohol, exercising regularly, and practicing relaxation techniques before bed can help reduce symptoms. In some cases, iron supplements may also be beneficial if a deficiency of this mineral is detected in the body.

Finally, circadian rhythm disorders are another type of sleep disorder that affects a person's biological clock. The human body is programmed to follow a natural sleep-wake cycle, known as the circadian rhythm, which usually coincides with the light-dark cycle of the day. However, in some people, this biological clock can be out of sync, causing them to have difficulty falling asleep or waking up at the right times.

A common example of a circadian rhythm disorder is "phase delay," which is when a person has difficulty falling asleep until very late at night and, as a result, finds it extremely difficult to wake up in the morning. This disorder is especially common in teenagers and young adults, and can interfere with their daily life, especially when they have to keep to early schedules, such as school or work. At the opposite extreme, some people experience "phase advance," which means they fall asleep very early and wake up in the middle of the night.

Intervention for circadian rhythm disorders usually involves gradually adjusting a person's sleep schedule so that it better aligns with the light-dark cycle. Light therapy, which involves exposure to bright light at certain times of the day, can help reset the biological clock. It's also important for people with this type of disorder to avoid exposure to bright light, especially light from electronic device screens, before bed, as this can interfere with the production of melatonin, a hormone that regulates sleep.

In conclusion, sleep disorders can severely impact a person's quality of life, but with the right interventions, it is possible to improve rest and, with it, overall well-being. From changes in sleep habits to more specialized therapies such as CBT or the use of devices such as CPAP, there are many options to help people overcome sleep challenges. Getting a good night's sleep is not only a biological necessity, but also a fundamental pillar for mental and physical health, and should not be underestimated.

Schizophrenia

Schizophrenia is a serious mental disorder that affects how a person thinks, feels, and behaves. People with schizophrenia often seem to have lost touch with reality, which can be very distressing for them and their family and friends. Schizophrenia can interfere with a person's ability to lead a normal life, as symptoms can make communication, social relationships, and daily functioning difficult.

One of the most well-known aspects of schizophrenia is psychotic symptoms, such as hallucinations and delusions. Hallucinations are perceptions that are not based in reality. A person may hear voices that are not there or see things that others do not see. These experiences can be frightening or confusing to the person experiencing them. For example, someone with schizophrenia may hear voices ordering them to do things or constantly swearing at them, which increases their anxiety and stress.

Delusions, on the other hand, are false beliefs that a person holds firmly, even though they have no basis in reality. A common example of a delusion is when a person believes that they are being stalked or watched, even though there is no evidence of this. They may also believe that they have special powers or that they are important figures, such as a famous person or deity. These delusions can lead to erratic behavior as the person acts on these beliefs, even though they may not make sense to others.

In addition to psychotic symptoms, schizophrenia can also affect thinking and how a person processes information. People with schizophrenia often experience what is called "thought disorganization." This means that their thoughts may be jumbled or incoherent, which can make it difficult for them to speak or follow a conversation. Sometimes, people with schizophrenia may jump from one topic to another with no apparent connection, or their words may be difficult to understand.

Another common feature of schizophrenia is "negative symptoms." These symptoms refer to a lack or decrease in certain skills or behaviors that are normally expected in a person. For example, someone with schizophrenia may show little or no emotion on their face or in their tone of voice, a phenomenon called "affective blunting." They may also have difficulty maintaining relationships, feeling motivated to do activities, or enjoying things they once enjoyed. Lack of interest and motivation can cause people with schizophrenia to isolate themselves, further exacerbating social and emotional problems.

The course of schizophrenia varies from person to person. Some people may have severe episodes, followed by recovery periods where symptoms are less intense. Other people may experience ongoing symptoms that interfere with their daily life. Schizophrenia often begins in the teen years or early adulthood, and early signs may include changes in behavior, social withdrawal, and a decline in academic or work performance.

Treating schizophrenia is critical to improving the quality of life for those who suffer from it. Fortunately, with the right treatment, many people with schizophrenia can lead more stable and functional lives. Treatment usually includes a combination of antipsychotic medications and therapy. Antipsychotics help reduce psychotic symptoms, such as hallucinations and delusions, by balancing chemicals in the brain that influence thinking and behavior. Although medications do not cure schizophrenia, they can control symptoms and help prevent relapses.

In addition to medication, psychological therapy is an important part of treatment. Cognitive behavioral therapy (CBT) can be especially helpful for people with schizophrenia, helping them identify and modify distorted or delusional thinking patterns. CBT can also teach coping skills, improve communication, and foster greater awareness of reality. Psychoeducation, involving the person with schizophrenia and their family, is also crucial. By educating both the patient and their loved ones about the illness, stigma is reduced, understanding is improved, and a stronger supportive environment is created.

An essential part of treatment is social and community support. People with schizophrenia often benefit from rehabilitation programs that teach them daily living skills, such as time management, self-care, and social interaction. These programs help people live more independently and reintegrate into the community. They may also participate in support groups, where they can share their experiences with others facing similar problems, giving them a sense of belonging and understanding.

The role of family and friends in the treatment of schizophrenia cannot be underestimated. People with schizophrenia need a strong support system, as the illness can be debilitating and difficult to manage alone. Families who educate themselves about schizophrenia and are involved in treatment can provide the emotional and practical support their loved ones need to cope with the challenges of the illness. It is also important for families and friends to maintain open communication with the health professionals who are involved in treatment, as this ensures that the patient receives the best care possible.

Despite advances in treatment, schizophrenia remains an illness that is often surrounded by misunderstanding and stigma. Many people mistakenly associate schizophrenia with violence or dangerous behaviour, but most people with schizophrenia are not violent. In fact, they are much more likely to be victims of violence or abuse due to their vulnerability. It is crucial that as a society we work to reduce the stigma associated with schizophrenia and other mental illnesses, as this can prevent people from seeking the treatment they need.

The outlook for people with schizophrenia has improved considerably in recent years thanks to advances in treatment and understanding of the illness. However, schizophrenia remains a chronic condition, meaning that most people will need lifelong treatment. Although this may seem daunting, it is important to remember that with the right support, people with schizophrenia can learn to manage their condition and lead more fulfilling lives.

In addition to traditional treatments, some complementary approaches may be helpful for people with schizophrenia. For example, occupational therapy can help them develop practical skills for daily living, while regular exercise and a balanced diet can improve their physical and mental wellbeing. Research is also being done into the use of new technologies, such as mobile apps, to help people manage their symptoms and receive real-time support.

It is essential for people with schizophrenia to receive treatment on an ongoing basis, even during periods when symptoms seem to be under control. Relapses are common in schizophrenia, and stopping treatment can increase the risk that symptoms will return or worsen. Treatment adherence, which means continuing to take medications as prescribed and attending therapy appointments, is key to maintaining stability and preventing relapses.

In summary, schizophrenia is a complex mental disorder that can profoundly impact a person's life, but it does not define who they are. With the right treatment, support from loved ones, and access to community resources, people with schizophrenia can learn to manage their symptoms and lead more balanced lives. It's important that we continue to advance our understanding of schizophrenia and reduce stigma, so that all people living with this condition receive the respect and support they deserve.

Substance Use Disorders

Substance use disorders are serious conditions that occur when drug or alcohol use begins to significantly interfere with a person's daily life. These disorders can range in severity from occasional problematic use to full-blown dependence, where the person feels they cannot function without the substance. It is a problem that affects people of all ages, genders, and social classes, and although it is a difficult topic to address, it is essential to understand it in order to treat it effectively.

One of the main signs of a substance use disorder is a loss of control over the use of the drug or alcohol. This means that the person uses more than they had planned, or that they continue to use the substance despite the problems it is causing in their life. Many times, someone with this disorder will try to stop using the substance but will find that they are unable to do so, leading to a cycle of dependence. This lack of control is a sign that the brain has become dependent on the substance and that the body may experience withdrawal symptoms if the person tries to stop using it.

Withdrawal symptoms are a major part of substance use disorder. When someone has been using a drug or consuming alcohol for a long period of time, their body and brain adjust to the presence of the substance. If they suddenly stop using it, the body may react with a variety of unpleasant symptoms, such as tremors, anxiety, insomnia, nausea, or even seizures in the most severe cases. These symptoms can be so intense that they cause the person to use the substance again to feel better, perpetuating the cycle of dependence.

Another aspect of substance use disorder is increasing tolerance. This means that over time, a person needs to consume more of the substance to feel the same effect as before. For example, someone who used to get drunk on just a few beers may find themselves drinking much more to reach the same level of intoxication. This tolerance can lead to excessive use, which increases the risk of physical harm, such as liver damage in the case of alcohol or breathing problems in the case of inhaled drug use.

The impact on the life of a person suffering from a substance use disorder is significant. These types of problems can affect relationships with family and friends, as the person may become more irritable, avoidant, or irresponsible due to their use. Work or school obligations are often affected, as the person may have difficulty concentrating or fulfilling their responsibilities due to the effects of the substance or hangover. It is also common for people with a substance use disorder to experience financial problems, as they spend a large portion of their money on the substance, often neglecting other needs.

In addition to the social and emotional effects, substance use disorders also have a devastating impact on physical health. Depending on the substance used, a variety of health problems can arise. Excessive alcohol use, for example, can cause liver damage, heart problems, and increase the risk of cancer. Using drugs such as cocaine or heroin can damage the heart, lungs, and brain, as well as increasing the risk of infections such as HIV or hepatitis if shared needles are used.

Treating substance use disorders is complex, but it is possible with the right approach. One of the first steps is acknowledging that there is a problem. This is often difficult, as many people who have a substance use disorder do not believe they need help, or they think they can control their use on their own. It is common for people to minimize the problem or blame external factors, such as stress or social pressure, for their substance use. However, the first step toward recovery is admitting that the use has become uncontrollable and is negatively affecting your life.

Once the problem is recognized, it is important to seek professional help. Treatment for substance use disorders often includes a combination of psychological therapy and, in some cases, medication. Cognitive behavioral therapy (CBT) is one form of treatment that has been shown to be effective for many people with substance use disorders. In CBT, people are helped to identify the thoughts and behaviors that contribute to their substance use and develop new ways to cope with them. Work is also done to increase motivation for change and set realistic goals for recovery.

Medication treatment can also be helpful, especially for alcohol or opioid use disorders. Medications such as naltrexone or buprenorphine can reduce cravings and help prevent relapse by blocking the effects of drugs on the brain. For alcohol, naltrexone can reduce the desire to drink by blocking the pleasure receptors that are activated by alcohol use. These medications are not a magic bullet, but they can be a useful tool within a broader treatment plan.

Social support is another key factor in the treatment of substance use disorders. Many people find that participating in support groups, such as Alcoholics Anonymous or Narcotics Anonymous, is very helpful in their recovery process. These groups provide an environment in which people can share their experiences and receive support from others facing similar problems. They can also help people feel less isolated and find a community of people who understand what they are going through.

It is important to note that recovery from a substance use disorder is an ongoing process. It is not uncommon for people to experience relapses, but the crucial thing is not to give up. Each relapse is an opportunity to learn more about the factors that trigger the use and adjust the treatment plan as needed. Patience and persistence are essential, both for the person in recovery and for their loved ones.

A key aspect of treating and preventing substance use disorders is addressing the underlying causes of the use. Many people turn to drugs or alcohol as a way to cope with stress, anxiety, depression, or other emotional problems. If these problems are not addressed, substance use is likely to continue or the person will turn to other forms of escape. Therefore, it is essential to treat both the substance use disorder and any mental health problems that may be present at the same time.

In summary, substance use disorders are complex problems that affect both the body and the mind. While overcoming such a disorder can be challenging, it is possible with the right treatment, support, and determination. The key is to recognize the problem, seek help, and be willing to work toward recovery, understanding that this process will take time and effort. With the right approach, people can regain control of their lives and learn to live without relying on substances to meet the challenges life throws at them.

Disruptive and Conduct Disorders in Children

Disruptive and conduct disorders in children are problems characterized by defiant, impulsive, or even aggressive behaviors that go beyond what is considered normal behavior for a child's age. These disorders can make it difficult for a child to follow rules, respect authority, or get along with peers and family members. Although many children go through stages of acting rebellious or disobedient, when these behaviors are persistent and severe, they could be signs of a conduct disorder.

One of the most common disorders in this category is oppositional defiant disorder, or ODD. Children with ODD are often argumentative and defiant toward authority figures, such as parents, teachers, or coaches. They often argue about everything, refuse to follow rules, and blame others for their mistakes or bad behavior. They can also be very sensitive and easily upset, which can cause them to overreact to situations that don't seem that serious to others. Although many children go through oppositional phases, in the case of ODD these behaviors occur so frequently and so intensely that they affect the well-being of the child and those around them.

Another major disorder within this group is conduct disorder. This is more severe than ODD, as children with this disorder are not only defiant, but may also display aggressive or destructive behaviors. Children with conduct disorder often deliberately and repeatedly break rules, such as lying, cheating, stealing, or even harming other people or property. They may be cruel to animals or peers, start physical fights, or threaten others. Conduct disorder can have a profound impact on a child's life, affecting their relationships with others and their ability to function at school or at home.

It's important to understand that children with these disorders aren't acting defiantly or aggressively because they simply want to cause trouble. Often, there are underlying factors that contribute to these behaviors, such as emotional difficulties, family problems, or stressful situations. Some children may be dealing with the impact of living in a chaotic or traumatic environment, while others may struggle to regulate their emotions or control their impulses due to differences in brain development. These disorders may also be linked to other mental health issues, such as anxiety or depression, further complicating the situation.

Treating disruptive and conduct disorders in children is essential to help them learn to manage their emotions and behaviors more effectively. One of the most commonly used approaches is behavioral therapy. In behavioral therapy, children learn to recognize their problematic behavior patterns and develop skills to control their impulses and reactions. Therapists also work with parents to teach them techniques they can use at home, such as setting clear rules applying consistent consequences, and reinforcing good behavior.

A crucial aspect of treatment is family involvement. In many cases, the family environment can play a major role in the development and maintenance of conduct disorders. For example, a child who lives in a home where there is a lot of tension, a lack of structure, or an inconsistent parenting style may have more difficulty learning to follow rules and control his or her emotions. Parent training programs are a valuable tool in these cases. Through these programs, parents learn to communicate more effectively with their children, set appropriate boundaries, and manage conflicts without resorting to physical punishment or constant arguments.

The educational approach is also key for children with disruptive and conduct disorders. At school, these children often have trouble following directions, paying attention, or completing assignments, which can lead to conflicts with teachers or a drop in academic performance. Teachers and school staff play an important role in supporting these children by setting clear expectations and providing a structured and predictable environment. Some schools offer special programs or intervention plans designed to help children with conduct problems improve their behavior and academic performance.

In some cases, medication may be part of the treatment for behavioral disorders, especially if the child also has other mental health problems, such as attention-deficit/hyperactivity disorder (ADHD) or anxiety. However, drug treatment is not the primary solution for these disorders. It is usually combined with therapy and changes in the child's environment for the best results. Medications may help reduce symptoms, such as impulsivity or aggression, but they do not address the underlying causes of the behavior.

The outlook for children with disruptive and conduct disorders can be positive if they receive early intervention and ongoing support. However, if these problems are not treated, they can continue into adolescence and adulthood, and increase the risk of more serious problems, such as substance abuse, delinquency, or difficulties maintaining healthy relationships. That's why it's crucial that parents, teachers, and health professionals work together to identify and treat these disorders as early as possible.

Prevention is also an important component of addressing disruptive and conduct disorders in children. Creating a stable home environment, fostering good communication, and establishing clear routines can help children develop a sense of security and responsibility. Parents can teach problem-solving skills, emotional control, and empathy from an early age, which can prevent the onset of conduct problems later in life.

In conclusion, disruptive and conduct disorders in children represent a challenge for both those affected and their families. These disorders not only interfere with a child's daily life, but can also have a long-lasting impact if not addressed appropriately. With the right treatment, which often includes a combination of behavioral therapy, family support, and educational strategies, children can learn to manage their emotions and behaviors, allowing them to lead more balanced and successful lives in the future.

Brief Psychotherapy

Brief psychotherapy is a therapeutic approach designed to treat emotional or psychological problems in a limited period of time. Unlike other types of therapy that can last for years, brief psychotherapy has a clear goal and focuses on solving specific problems in a set number of sessions, usually ranging from 8 to 20. This type of therapy is based on the idea that long-term treatment is not necessary to achieve significant changes in a person's well-being. Rather, with a structured and targeted approach, it is possible to achieve noticeable improvements in a short period of time.

One of the key features of brief psychotherapy is that it is very goal-focused. From the beginning, the therapist and patient work together to identify what are the most pressing issues they want to address and what goals they want to achieve. This process helps focus the sessions, preventing the therapy from becoming too general or scattered. For example, if a patient comes in with anxiety problems at work, the goal might be to develop strategies to reduce that anxiety in specific situations, such as presentations or meetings.

Another key aspect of brief psychotherapy is that it is often very active and therapist-led. Rather than simply listening and providing space for reflection, the therapist in this approach tends to be more direct about suggesting solutions, offering feedback, and working with the patient to practice new skills. This does not mean that therapy becomes a series of advice, but rather it is about guiding the patient to find practical and applicable ways to cope with their problems. The therapist's role is to help the patient see situations from different perspectives and to effectively encourage changes in their behavior or thinking.

One of the theories behind brief psychotherapy is that people often have the resources within themselves to solve their problems, but they may need help figuring out how to use them. Rather than delving into a person's past or exploring all the root causes of their problems, this approach focuses on finding solutions and ways to move forward. This is particularly helpful for people who are looking for concrete outcomes and who are not interested in a lengthy exploration of their personal history.

Although brief psychotherapy can treat a variety of problems, it tends to be most effective when used to address issues that are specific and clearly defined. Problems such as anxiety, stress, mild depression, relationship difficulties, or work conflicts may be ideal for this type of approach. For example, a patient who is dealing with emotional distress due to a recent breakup might benefit from brief psychotherapy, as the goal would be to process the emotions associated with the breakup and find healthy ways to move on, without needing to explore their past relationship history in detail.

A common approach within brief psychotherapy is cognitive behavioural therapy (CBT). CBT is based on the idea that our thoughts influence our emotions and behaviours, and that by changing our thinking patterns, we can change how we feel and how we act. In the context of brief psychotherapy, CBT is used to identify dysfunctional thoughts that are contributing to the patient's problems and then replace them with more helpful and positive thoughts. This process involves actively working to recognise negative thinking patterns and develop new ways of interpreting situations.

For example, if someone is constantly worried about what others think of them, therapy would work to identify those automatic thoughts, such as "They must think I'm incompetent," and then question them. What evidence is there that this is true? Is there another way to interpret the situation? Through this type of questioning, the patient can begin to develop a new way of thinking that causes less anxiety and allows them to act more confidently in social situations.

Another important feature of brief psychotherapy is that, as it is a short-term treatment, it often includes tasks or "homework" that patients must complete outside of sessions. These tasks are designed to help the patient practice the new skills they are learning in therapy and apply them to their daily lives. For example, if someone is working on improving their self-esteem, the therapist might suggest that the patient make a daily list of their accomplishments or try speaking up in a meeting at work, something they would normally find awkward. These tasks not only reinforce what they have learned in therapy, but they also help the patient see concrete progress between sessions.

Brief psychotherapy is not only helpful because it is effective in a short period of time, but it can also be more accessible to many people. For those who have busy schedules or who cannot commit to long-term therapy, this approach provides a way to get help and improve their well-being without the need to commit a significant amount of time. Additionally, it can be more cost-effective compared to long-term therapy, as the number of sessions is limited.

However, it is important to note that brief psychotherapy is not suitable for all psychological problems. Complex or long-standing disorders, such as personality disorders or deep trauma, may require a longer exploration and a different therapeutic approach. In such cases, a longer-term therapy that allows for a deeper process may be more beneficial. However, even in these cases, brief psychotherapy can be a starting point to address specific problems before moving on to longer-term treatment.

One of the main advantages of brief psychotherapy is that it encourages the patient's independence. Because time is limited, the patient learns from the beginning that he or she has an active role in his or her recovery. As the sessions progress, the patient is expected to acquire the tools necessary to manage his or her problems more effectively without constantly depending on the therapist. This sense of autonomy can be very empowering and helps to ensure that the changes achieved in therapy are maintained in the long term.

Despite its limited duration, brief psychotherapy can have a lasting impact on a person's life. Many people find that by learning new ways to cope with their problems in a relatively short period of time, they are able to apply those same principles to other areas of their lives, even after therapy has ended. This is especially true in approaches like CBT, where the skills learned, such as identifying negative thoughts and modifying behaviors, can continue to be useful long after the sessions have concluded.

In summary, brief psychotherapy is an effective and accessible option for people looking to resolve specific problems in a short period of time. With a structured, goal-focused approach and active participation from both therapist and patient, this form of therapy can make significant changes in people's lives without the need for a long-term commitment. Although it is not suitable for everyone, for many, brief psychotherapy offers a practical and effective way to improve their emotional and mental well-being.

Therapeutic Relationship and Alliance with the Patient

The therapeutic relationship is one of the most important elements in any type of psychological treatment. This relationship refers to the bond that is formed between the therapist and the patient during the therapy process. It is a connection based on trust, respect, and collaboration, and is essential for the success of any therapeutic intervention. Without a good therapeutic relationship, it is much more difficult for the patient to feel comfortable opening up and sharing their thoughts and emotions. In addition, this relationship is key for the patient to be able to move forward with the treatment and feel motivated to work on their problems.

When we talk about the therapeutic alliance, we are specifically referring to one part of this relationship, which is the agreement between the patient and the therapist about the goals of the therapy and the means to achieve them. This alliance implies that both parties are aligned as to what they want to achieve and how they are going to do it. If the patient and the therapist do not agree on these aspects, there may be problems in the progress of the therapy, since they will not be working in the same direction. That is why it is so important to establish a good therapeutic alliance from the beginning, where both are clear about what is expected to be achieved and how they are going to work to achieve it.

One of the keys to building a good therapeutic relationship is for the therapist to be empathetic and understanding. This means that the therapist should strive to see the world from the patient's perspective, trying to understand how they feel and what they are experiencing. Empathy is not the same as sympathy; it is not about feeling sorry for the patient, but about acknowledging and validating their emotions. When a patient feels that their therapist truly understands them, they are more likely to feel safe and confident to talk about their deeper issues. This sense of being understood is an essential part of effective therapy.

Another important aspect in the therapeutic relationship is trust. For therapy to work, the patient must feel comfortable enough to share aspects of his or her life that he or she may never have discussed with anyone else. This trust is not earned immediately, but is built over time. The therapist must be consistent, honest, and transparent so that the patient feels that he or she can be trusted. Often, the simple act of listening without judgment can be enough for the patient to begin to open up. Confidentiality is a crucial component in this trust, as the patient must be assured that everything he or she shares in therapy will be kept private.

The therapeutic relationship must also be collaborative. Although the therapist has the training and skills to guide the process, therapy is a team effort. The patient plays an active role in his or her own treatment, as he or she knows best his or her own thoughts and feelings. The therapist is not there to give answers or solutions, but to help the patient discover them for themselves. When the patient feels part of the process, he or she is more likely to engage with the treatment and do the work necessary to get better.

Sometimes patients come to therapy with unrealistic expectations, expecting the therapist to have all the answers or that therapy will be a quick fix to their problems. This is where the therapeutic alliance plays a crucial role. The therapist must work with the patient to set clear and realistic expectations from the beginning. For example, if a patient hopes to overcome a deep depression in just a couple of sessions, the therapist must explain that the process will take longer and will require effort on both sides. At the same time, it is important for the therapist to recognize the patient's goals and try to work with him or her to achieve them as effectively as possible.

Breakups in the therapeutic relationship are inevitable at times, but they are not necessarily a bad thing. Sometimes a patient may become frustrated or misunderstand something the therapist said, which can create tension in the relationship. Rather than ignoring these moments, it is important for the therapist and patient to talk openly about them. Resolving these breakups can strengthen the therapeutic relationship and increase trust. By learning how to manage conflict in the therapeutic relationship, the patient can also learn valuable skills for managing conflict in other areas of their life.

The therapeutic relationship also includes setting clear boundaries. The therapist should maintain a professional distance, even if warm and understanding. This distance is important because it allows the therapist to maintain an objective perspective, which is essential to providing effective treatment. In addition, it helps the patient feel safe, knowing that the relationship is clearly defined and that the therapist is there to help them, but not to become personally involved in their life. Setting these boundaries from the beginning is essential to avoid misunderstandings and maintain a healthy therapeutic relationship.

An additional element to consider is the individualization of the therapeutic relationship. Not all patients are the same and what works for one may not work for another. A good therapist is able to adapt to the needs and personalities of each patient. Some patients may need more emotional support, while others prefer a more structured and direct approach. The therapist's ability to adjust to the patient's preferences without losing sight of the goals of the therapy is key to the success of the treatment.

The therapeutic relationship is also affected by the cultural context and life experiences of the patient. Patients come from different cultures, religions, and family backgrounds, and all of these influence how they view therapy and what they expect from it. A therapist who is sensitive to these factors can build a better relationship with the patient and offer more appropriate treatment. For example, some patients may come from cultures where talking about emotional problems is not common or even viewed with suspicion. In these cases, the therapist must be especially careful and respectful not to impose his or her own ideas, but to work with the patient from his or her cultural perspective.

In summary, the therapeutic relationship and alliance with the patient are the foundation of effective therapy. This relationship is built on trust, empathy, mutual respect, and an active collaboration between therapist and patient. It is through this connection that the patient can feel safe enough to explore their problems and work on solutions. While therapy can involve many different techniques and approaches, it is the quality of the relationship between therapist and patient that ultimately determines the success of the treatment.

Treatment of Attention Deficit Hyperactivity Disorder (ADHD)

Attention deficit hyperactivity disorder, better known as ADHD, is a condition that affects both children and adults and is characterized by problems with maintaining attention, hyperactivity, and impulsivity. People with ADHD often have difficulty concentrating on tasks, may act without thinking about the consequences, and often seem to be constantly on the move or restless. This disorder can significantly affect academic performance, work performance, and personal relationships, so it is important to seek treatment early.

Treatment for ADHD typically involves a combination of interventions, which may include medication, behavioral therapy, education, and support for those affected. Each case of ADHD is unique, so approaches should be tailored to each person's individual needs.

Medication treatment is one of the most common ways to treat ADHD. Stimulant medications, such as methylphenidate or amphetamines, are the most commonly prescribed and have been shown to be effective for many people. These drugs help improve concentration, increase attention, and reduce impulsive behaviors. Despite being called stimulants, in people with ADHD these medications actually have a calming effect. They work by increasing the activity of certain neurotransmitters in the brain, such as dopamine and norepinephrine, which are responsible for attention and impulse control.

However, not everyone responds to medications in the same way. Some people may experience side effects, such as loss of appetite, trouble sleeping, or irritability. In those cases, doctors may adjust dosages or try other types of medications, such as nonstimulants, which can also help manage ADHD symptoms. Additionally, medications alone are not enough to address all aspects of the disorder, so it is critical to combine this approach with other types of treatment.

Behavioral therapy is a crucial part of ADHD treatment. In this therapy, the patient learns to manage his or her problematic behaviors through techniques that reinforce self-control and improve organization. For children, behavioral therapy may involve a system of rewards and consequences. For example, parents can use behavior charts or graphs to reward good behaviors and set clear consequences for inappropriate behaviors. This approach not only helps children learn to regulate their behaviors, but also teaches important daily living skills, such as planning tasks, staying organized, and setting priorities.

For adults with ADHD, behavioral therapy focuses more on creating strategies to manage the demands of work, relationships, and daily responsibilities. Often, work is done on developing skills for time management, problem-solving, and decision-making. Adults with ADHD may have trouble completing long tasks or following routines, so in therapy they are taught to break down large tasks into smaller, manageable steps and to set reminders or alarms to make sure things get done on time.

Educational support is another important tool for treating ADHD, especially in children and adolescents. Teachers and parents should be involved in the treatment process so that children receive the help they need both at home and at school. Often, children with ADHD have difficulty paying attention in the classroom, which affects their academic performance. For this reason, it is common for accommodations to be implemented in the school environment, such as giving them more time to complete tests, allowing them to take frequent breaks, or seating them in a place where there are fewer distractions.

Parent training is also essential in the treatment of ADHD. Parents of children with this disorder may feel frustrated or overwhelmed when trying to manage their children's behaviors. Training teaches parents how to respond positively and effectively to problem behaviors, how to set clear and consistent rules, and how to use positive reinforcement to encourage good behaviors. This type of training can make a big difference in the family environment, reducing stress and improving communication between parents and children.

An important aspect of ADHD treatment is education about the disorder, both for those affected and their families. Understanding how ADHD works and how it affects behavior can help reduce the guilt and frustration often felt by both those with the disorder and their loved ones. Knowing that ADHD is a neurological condition and not a problem of laziness or lack of willpower can be a relief and may open the door to finding more effective solutions.

ADHD treatment may also include lifestyle changes. Exercising regularly, maintaining a balanced diet, and having a stable sleep routine can all improve ADHD symptoms. Exercise, in particular, can be very beneficial for people with ADHD, as it helps reduce hyperactivity and improves concentration. Physical activities such as running, swimming, or cycling can release extra energy and calm the mind, making it easier to focus on other tasks.

Another component that can be helpful in treating ADHD is cognitive behavioral therapy. This form of therapy focuses on changing negative thoughts and beliefs that may be affecting a person's ability to manage ADHD symptoms. For example, an adult with ADHD who always feels like a "failure" because he or she can't finish tasks on time can learn to identify these negative thoughts and replace them with more realistic, positive thoughts. Additionally, cognitive behavioral therapy teaches practical skills to improve organization, planning, and decision-making, which can be especially helpful for those who struggle with a lack of structure or chaos in their daily lives.

It's important to note that treating ADHD is not a quick or easy process. Because it is a chronic condition, symptoms may persist throughout life, and treatment may need to be adjusted as a person grows or their circumstances change. However, with proper treatment and a comprehensive approach that combines medication, therapy, and support, many people with ADHD can lead full and successful lives.

In summary, ADHD treatment involves a combination of approaches including medication, behavioral therapy, educational support, and lifestyle changes. Every person with ADHD is different, so it's critical to tailor treatment to each patient's individual needs. With the right treatment, people with ADHD can learn to manage their symptoms and overcome the challenges they face in their daily lives. Although the road can be long and sometimes frustrating, early intervention and a sustained approach can make a big difference in the lives of those with the disorder.

Ethics and Legal Considerations in Clinical Psychology

Ethics and legal considerations are essential elements in the practice of clinical psychology. Clinical psychologists work with people seeking help for their emotional and mental problems, so it is critical that they maintain high ethical standards to ensure that their work is respectful, safe, and responsible. At the same time, they must be aware of the laws and regulations that govern their profession in order to avoid legal problems and protect both patients and themselves. This chapter will address how ethical principles and legal considerations influence the daily work of a clinical psychologist and why they are so important in the mental health field.

One of the most important ethical principles in clinical psychology is that of confidentiality. When a person sees a psychologist, they share very personal information, often about their innermost thoughts, emotions, and life experiences. This information must be treated as discreetly as possible. Psychologists have an ethical and legal obligation to maintain the confidentiality of their patients, which means that they cannot reveal anything that is discussed in sessions without the patient's consent, except in specific circumstances, such as when there is a risk of imminent harm to the patient or others. This creates a safe environment for people to speak openly without fear of their information being shared with others.

However, there are situations in which confidentiality may be limited. For example, if a patient discloses that he or she intends to harm himself or herself or another person, the psychologist has a legal and ethical responsibility to intervene to prevent that harm. This may involve breaking confidentiality to notify authorities or a close family member, depending on the case. Although this situation may be difficult for both the patient and the therapist, the protection of life and well-being is always a priority. In these cases, the psychologist must clearly and compassionately communicate the reasons behind the decision to break confidentiality, so that the patient understands that he or she is acting in his or her best interest.

Another important aspect of ethics in clinical psychology is informed consent. Before starting any treatment, psychologists must ensure that their patients understand what the therapeutic process will involve and what they can expect from it. This includes explaining the potential risks, benefits, and alternatives of the treatment. The patient must give consent to participate in therapy with full knowledge of what it entails. This principle protects the rights of the patient and ensures that they are making informed decisions about their own well-being. If the patient is a minor or otherwise unable to make decisions for themselves, consent must be obtained from a legal guardian.

Informed consent is not just a formal requirement, but an ongoing part of the therapeutic process. As therapy progresses, psychologists must ensure that patients continue to understand and accept the procedures. If the psychologist introduces new techniques or changes the treatment approach, it is essential that the patient is aware of and accepts these changes. In this way, informed consent becomes a tool for maintaining an open and collaborative relationship between therapist and patient.

Professional competence is another fundamental ethical principle in clinical psychology. Psychologists must work only within their area of competence, that is, they must have the necessary training and experience to treat the problems presented by their patients. If a psychologist does not have the appropriate skills to handle a particular case, he or she is obliged to refer the patient to another professional who is better qualified to care for him or her. This not only ensures that the patient receives the best possible treatment, but also protects the psychologist from falling into errors or malpractice. Furthermore, competence implies a continuous commitment to updating knowledge and skills. Psychology is a field that is constantly evolving, and it is the psychologist's responsibility to keep up to date with the latest developments in research and treatment.

The relationship between the psychologist and the patient must be free of any kind of exploitation. This means that the psychologist must never use his or her position of power to obtain personal benefits at the expense of the patient's well-being. This includes avoiding any kind of dual relationship, which is when the therapist maintains a relationship outside of therapy with the patient, whether of a social, financial or intimate nature. Dual relationships can interfere with the therapeutic process and negatively affect the patient, as they can cloud the therapist's judgment or create conflicts of interest.

Legal considerations in clinical psychology are also important. In many countries, clinical psychologists must be licensed or registered with a regulatory body. This licensing process ensures that the psychologist meets certain standards of education, training, and ethics before being allowed to practice. In addition, psychologists must follow local laws regarding the practice of psychology, which may include requirements regarding the handling of patient records, the conditions under which confidentiality can be broken, and rules regarding private practice and advertising of psychological services.

Documentation is another essential legal aspect. Psychologists must keep accurate and detailed records of sessions with their patients. These records may include notes on the patient's progress, treatments applied, and any relevant incidents that occur during therapy. Documentation is not only useful for tracking treatment progress, but also protects the psychologist in the event of a lawsuit. Records must be handled confidentially and stored securely to protect patient privacy.

In some cases, clinical psychologists may be involved in legal proceedings, either as expert witnesses or as evaluators of an individual's mental health. In these situations, they must ensure that they follow ethical principles and act impartially and professionally. Although the psychologist may be assisting the judicial system in making important decisions, their primary responsibility remains to the patient and their well-being.

In short, ethics and legal considerations are the foundation upon which the practice of clinical psychology is built. Psychologists must act ethically at all times, protecting the confidentiality of their patients, obtaining informed consent, and ensuring that they are working within their area of expertise. At the same time, they must comply with the laws and regulations that govern the practice of psychology to ensure that their work is legal and safe. These guidelines not only protect patients, but also ensure that psychologists can provide the best possible treatment in a responsible and respectful manner.